In the friendly forest of Acadia National Park, there lived a little bird named Chick-a-dee-dee-dee. He was a member of the Black-Capped family and lived in a warm nest with his six brothers and sisters.

When Chick-a-dee-dee-dee was only two weeks old, he learned to fly. It wasn't long before he was fluttering through the tall pine trees, exploring the forest, and making new friends.

Friends like Rufus Moose, Buzzy Beaver, and Franny Fox.

Chick-a-dee-dee-dee was a happy little bird indeed. He spent his summer days feasting on scrumptious leaf beetles, tasty weevils, and yummy saw-flies.

He liked to take baths in rain puddles and teeter on the tippy-tops of trees.

One August morning, Chick-a-dee-dee-dee went on a camping trip with his Mom and Dad, and all his brothers and sisters . . . cousins, aunts and uncles, and grandparents on both sides.
They flew to the top of Cadillac Mountain, where they camped out in some low lying bushes. They had a splendid time.

It was also the first time Chick-a-dee-dee-dee ever saw humans. He thought they were strange looking. They came in all shapes and sizes. They didn't have feathers or wings like he had, or antlers like Rufus Moose, or even a tail like Franny Fox. In fact, they were like nothing he had ever seen before. He was afraid of them at first, until his Dad told him that humans were kind creatures who liked to feed birds.

By the time the flock was ready to fly home,
Chick-a-dee-dee-dee had become quite daring.

He had learned the secret of taking food out of human hands.
He would land butterfly-lightly on their palms, then gently
peck up the tiny bits of sunflower seeds. Yes, Chick-a-dee-dee-
dee was no longer afraid of humans, for they had become his
friends.

Fall came, and the change in temperature turned the green leaves into woodfairy colors. Red-red, orange-orange, and golden yellow leaves twirled in the cool air, dancing on wind whispers until they softly made a blanket on the forest floor.

All the forest animals were busy preparing for the winter.

Franny Fox was digging a new den.

Charlie Chipmunk was storing acorns.

And Chick-a-dee-dee-dee's family was getting ready for their trip to Portland, where they would winter in Deering Oaks Park.

By now, Chick-a-dee-dee-dee was almost six months old. He was just a kiss over five inches long and had a wingspread of nearly eight inches. He was a handsome bird, with a short bill, a black cap and bib, and marshmallow-white cheeks.

Chick-a-dee-dee-dee had learned how to eat upside down. He could do flitter furls and flying flips, and flutter flutters.

But even though he could do all this, Chick-a-dee-dee-dee had become an unhappy bird. He was unhappy because he didn't feel special.

His friend Rufus Moose was special because of his great strength and size and stately antlers.

His friend Franny Fox was special because of her sharp sense of smell and crafty cleverness.

His friend Buzzy Beaver was special because he was a superior swimmer and builder of beautiful dams.

One day, as he was sitting on a tree branch, too sad to sing songs, Franny Fox asked him what was the matter.

"My, my," sighed Franny Fox after Chick-a-dee-dee-dee told her why he was so sad. She groomed her long red tail and thought and thought of a way to help her little feathered friend.

"I know!" she barked at last. "The Great Gray Owl! He is the wisest winged wizard of the woods. I'm sure he could help you be special."
"But where does he live?" chirped Chick-a-dee-dee-dee.
"Far, far away," Franny told him, "in the beautiful woods of Baxter State Park."

Chick-a-dee-dee-dee decided to go to Baxter State Park. He talked it over with his parents. They were sad about his leaving, but understood why it was important for him to go. His Dad told him the best route to take. His Mom told him he could spend the winter with the Brown-Capped Chickadee family. She said they were very friendly and lived at the entrance of Baxter State Park.

So, the very next day, as Chick-a-dee-dee-dee's family flew South in a large flock to Portland, Chick-a-dee-dee-dee headed North in search of the Great Gray Owl.

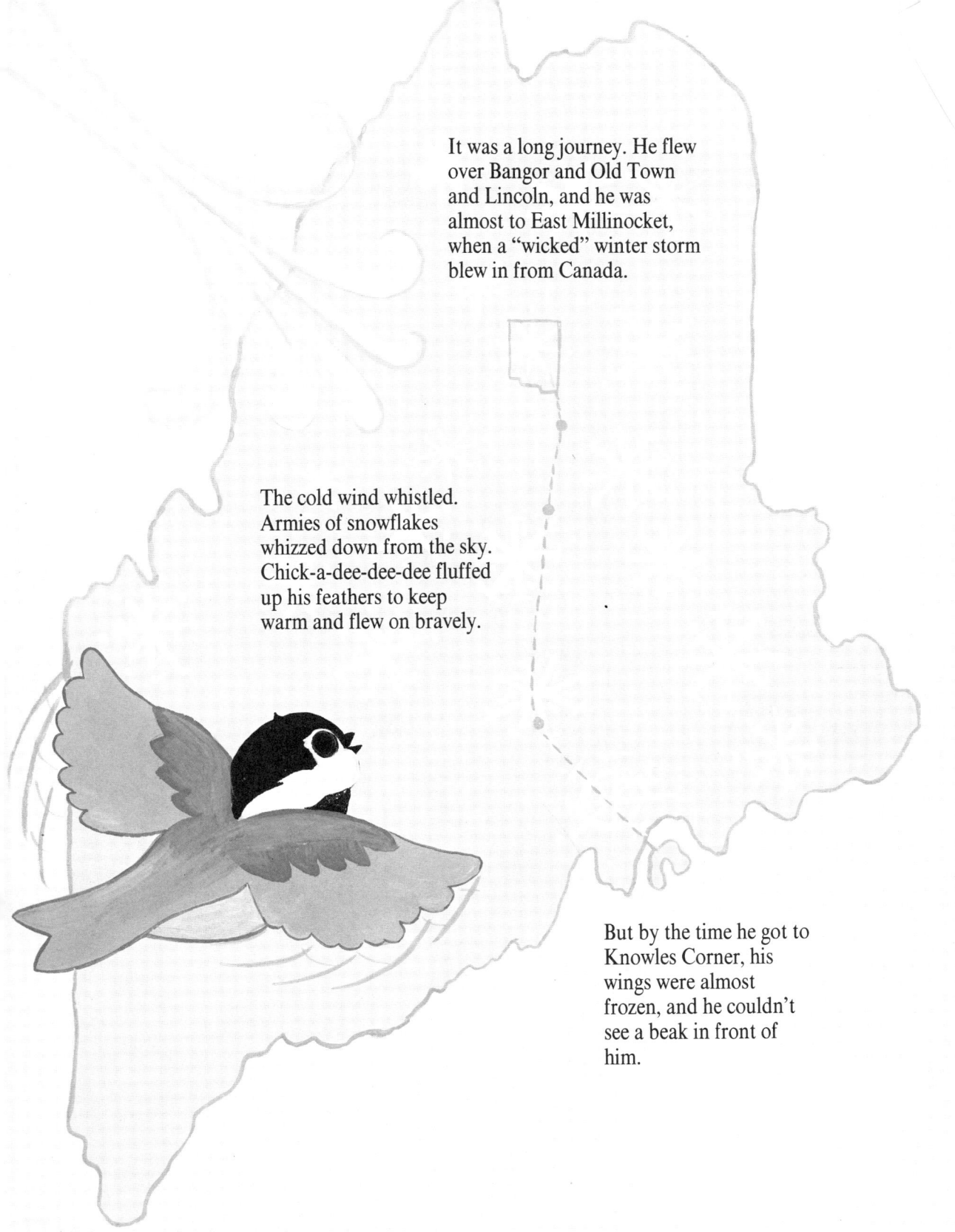

It was a long journey. He flew over Bangor and Old Town and Lincoln, and he was almost to East Millinocket, when a "wicked" winter storm blew in from Canada.

The cold wind whistled. Armies of snowflakes whizzed down from the sky. Chick-a-dee-dee-dee fluffed up his feathers to keep warm and flew on bravely.

But by the time he got to Knowles Corner, his wings were almost frozen, and he couldn't see a beak in front of him.

Poor Chick-a-dee-dee-dee was blizzard cold, tummy hungry, and very, very lonely.

It just so happened, at that very moment, a kindly human was shoveling his driveway.

As soon as he saw Chick-a-dee-dee-dee in the snowbank, he carefully picked him up and brought him inside his house.

Chick-a-dee-dee-dee had never been inside a human nest before. So, after warming up in front of a toasty fire, he hopped about.

In the middle of the nest was the strangest looking tree he had ever seen. It had shiny things hanging on its branches and had firefly lights that went blink, blink, blink.

He was puzzled indeed. But because he was so tummy hungry, he fluttered up to one of the branches, and topsy-turvy, feasted on a string of plump red cranberries.

By morning, the storm was over.
The air was crisp.
The sun smiled brightly.

The kindly human took Chick-a-dee-dee-dee outside and set him free. Chick-a-dee-dee-dee said "thank you" by doing a flutter bow. Then he flew away on a gentle Northwest wind, toward Baxter State Park.

Chick-a-dee-dee-dee reached Baxter by noontime. At the Park's entrance, he stopped to have lunch with the Brown-Capped Chick-a-dee family. His Mom was right, they were very friendly. And they told him just where the Great Gray Owl lived.

So, after a hearty lunch of pine cone seeds, he flew to the home of the Great Gray Owl.

"Who-oo-oo-oo are you-oo-oo?" asked the Great Gray Owl, in a deep booming voice.

Chick-a-dee-dee-dee felt itty-bitty-small as he looked up at the HUGE owl. The owl was ash gray with smokey shaded feathers. His head was big and round, and his eyes were fire-yellow. He had silvery feathered rings around his eyes and a charcoal black spot right in the middle of his chin.

Chick-a-dee-dee-dee bowed in front of the wisest winged wizard in the woods, then fluffed up his feathers and bravely chirped, "My name is Chick-a-dee-dee-dee, and I want to be special."

"You-oo-oo ar-ar-are," said the Great Gray Owl.

Chick-a-dee-dee-dee hopped one step closer and asked, "I am?"

The Great Gray Owl blinked his large yellow eyes, then told him . . .

"Even in the winter
We find you here at home,
In the pretty pine trees,
Among the tassels and cones.

"A hardy, handsome midget,
Who helps our forest trees
By eating nasty insects
That hurt the lovely leaves.

"Your flocks are large in number
And friendly as can be.
Maine humans love your sweet call
Of Chick-a-dee-dee-dee.

"So flutter on my feathered friend,
And let it now be heard,
That you are very special,
You are the Maine State Bird!"

Chick-a-dee-dee-dee swelled up with pride. Being the Maine State Bird was a great, great honor, indeed.

After thanking the Great Gray Owl, he returned to the Brown-Capped Chick-a-dee family. His Mom had told him to spend the winter with them, and he did just that.

When a spring wind finally arrived, Chick-a-dee-dee-dee said "goodbye" to his good friends and began his journey home.

He flew over Old Town and Bangor and Ellsworth, and by the time he reached the friendly forest of Acadia National Park, it was April.

Meanwhile, his Mom and Dad, and all his brothers and sisters . . . cousins, aunts and uncles, and grandparents on both sides, had also returned to the forest.

With them had come a beautiful chickadee named Phoebe. She was from a Portland Black-Capped family, and like everyone else, she thought Chick-a-dee-dee-dee was very brave.

Now, April being the month of love, it was only fitting that beautiful Phoebe and the brave Chick-a-dee-dee-dee, pair off. Together they began to build a nest in an old tree stump.

"Fee
    bee

    Fee
        bee"

they called to each other as they built their nest with fluffy feathers, puff hair, warm fur, and soft moss they found on the forest floor.

After nine days of hard work, the nest was finally finished. It was snug-a-bug warm and truly a Chickadee work of art. Phoebe made herself comfortable and, for a whole week, laid an egg a day.

They were lovely white eggs with reddish-brown freckles.

For the next twelve days she and Chick-a-dee-dee-dee took turns sitting on their precious eggs.

Finally, the baby birds hatched out of their warm shells, and Phoebe and Chick-a-dee-dee-dee became parents. Chick-a-dee-dee-dee puffed up proudly as he watched his sons and daughters play peek-a-boo in their nest.

When they were old enough he would teach them to fly, find beetles, and weevils, and sawflies.

He would tell them of the kindness of humans and of his journey North in search of the Great Gray Owl.

But most important, he would tell them why
they would always be special:

"Even in the winter
We find you here at home,
In the pretty pine trees,
Among the tassels and cones.

"A hardy, handsome midget,
Who helps our forest trees
By eating nasty insects
That hurt the lovely leaves.

"Your flocks are large in number
And friendly as can be.
Maine humans love your sweet call
Of Chick-a-dee-dee-dee.

"So flutter on my feathered friend,
And let it now be heard,
That you are very special,
You are the Maine State Bird!"

According to the *Maine Revised Statutes Annotated,* vol. 2, pg. 70, it is stated — "The State Bird shall be the Chickadee." This law was enacted in 1959.